The Giant Panda at Home

The Giant Panda at Home

MARGARET RAU

with drawings by Eva Hülsmann

ALFRED A. KNOPF · New York

For Kristen

This is a Borzoi Book, published by Alfred A. Knopf, Inc.

Text Copyright © 1977 by Margaret Rau. Illustrations Copyright © 1977 by Alfred A. Knopf, Inc. All rights reserved under International and Pan-American Copyright Conventions. Published in the United States by Alfred A. Knopf, Inc., New York, and simultaneously in Canada by Random House of Canada Limited, Toronto. Distributed by Random House, Inc., New York. Manufactured in the United States of America.

Library of Congress Cataloging in Publication Data
Rau, Margaret. The giant panda at home. Bibliography: p. 74 Summary: Introduces the physical characteristics and habits of the giant panda describing its role in the ecology of its natural environment in China and its past and present relationship to its human neighbors. 1. Giant panda— Juvenile literature.
[1. Giant panda. 2. Pandas] I. Hülsmann, Eva. II. Title. QL737.C27R38 599'.74443 76-40332
ISBN 0-394-83248-5 ISBN 0-394-93248-X lib. bdg.

Map on page 2 is by Ed Malsberg

Contents

Foreword *vii*

Prologue: The Home of the Giant Panda 3

1: Finding Mates 6

2: Wanderer 13

3: Alpine Meadows 23

4: The Cubs Are Born 33

5: Wilderness Tragedy 41

6: The Downward Trek 48

7: Growing Up 54

8: The Separation 59

Epilogue 67

Bibliography 74

Index 77

Foreword

TO MANY PEOPLE, especially those who have seen the giant panda in zoos around the world, the animal seems like a lovable toy come to life, an animated childhood fantasy. Its many near-human characteristics and its sad clown face have fostered an all too anthropomorphic interpretation of its behavior.

It was my wish in this book to remove the panda from the artificial atmosphere of the zoo and return it to its native habitat, the mountain wilderness of Szechuan Province in far western China. My aim in doing this was to bring out the animal's basic nature as it is expressed in the wild.

Since no creature can exist by itself, I have tried as well to re-create a total picture of the wilderness through which the panda roams. This includes descriptions of those other rare creatures whose habitat it shares.

Much of my information about the panda comes from the 1974 *Acta Zoologica Sinica*, the journal of the Peking Zoological Gardens, which I obtained during a recent visit to the Peking zoo and subsequently translated. The information in this journal includes not only the care, feeding, and breeding of zoo pandas, but also the details of several expeditions to Szechuan's Wanglang Preserve to observe the animal in its native home.

I have also had recourse to English translations of the writings of Ernst Schaefer, a German naturalist who in the 1930s spent some time studying the fauna and flora of the region. And I have read voluminously from other explorers, naturalists, and hunters who in previous years ventured into the mountainous areas of far western China. For those who are interested in more complete scientific and historical evidence available on the giant panda, I have included in the Epilogue additional technical information about the panda's evolution and details about the history of man's encounters with—and effect on—the panda in its natural habitat.

Using all sources available I have attempted to depict as faithfully as possible the varied activities and behavior of the giant panda at home. It is my hope that this book may serve as a tribute to this strange and wonderful animal.

The Giant Panda at Home

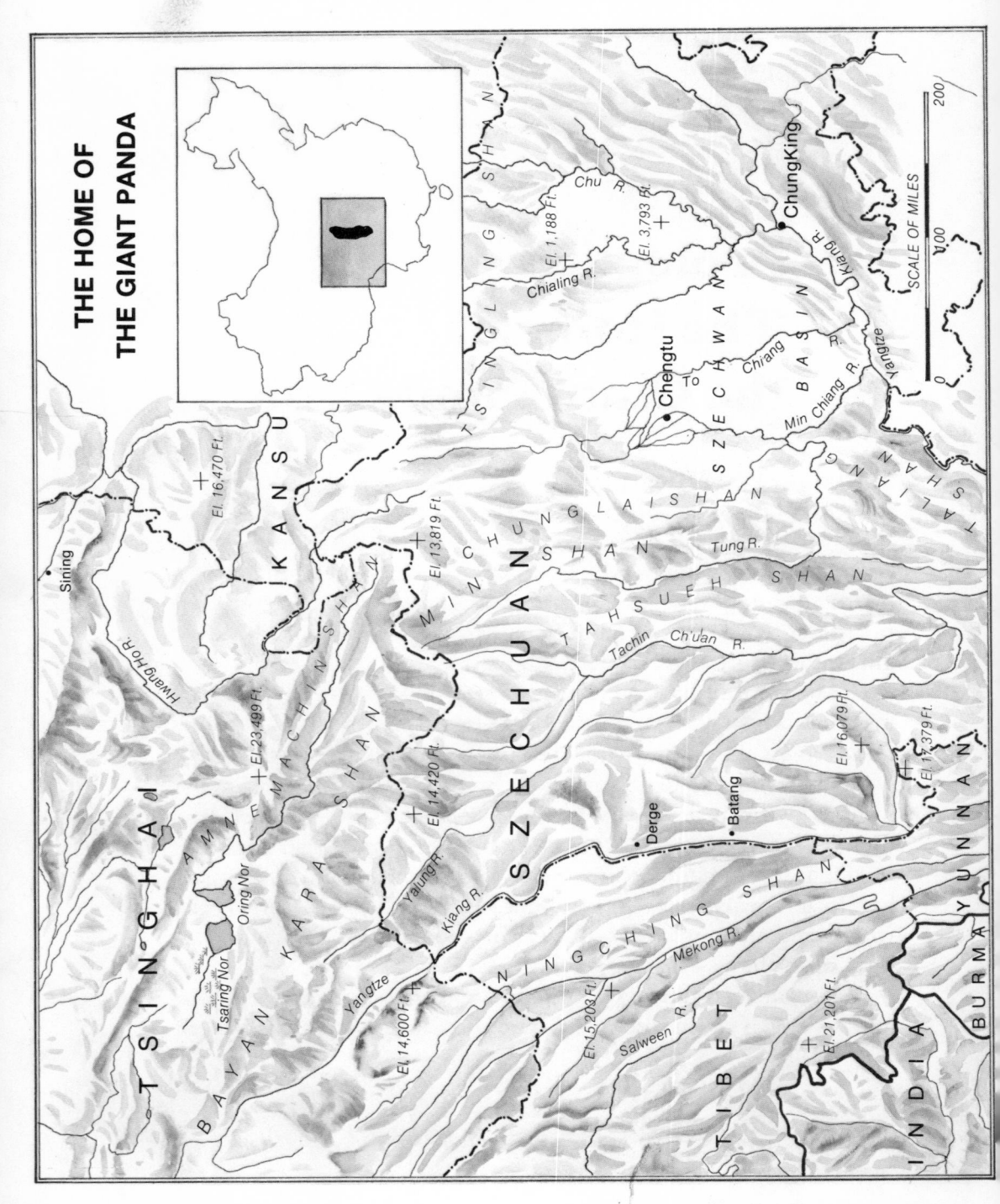

THE HOME OF
THE GIANT PANDA

Prologue:
The Home of
the Giant Panda

THE HOME of the giant panda lies in some of the wildest country in the world—the towering mountainous region of far western China. Here above the rich, low-lying farmlands of the Szechuan basin rises a broken wilderness cut by deep ravines and almost perpendicular slopes. Ridge after ridge mounts upward to the highest peaks, some 24,000 feet above sea level, brooding beneath their glistening white caps of perpetual snow.

Heavy rainfall has made the ravines and lower slopes of the mountains lush with greenery. They are crisscrossed with streams and rivulets that plunge down fiercely in foaming cataracts and waterfalls flashing with spray. A broad forest belt circles the mountains. In it are many kinds of deciduous trees, which lose their leaves in winter—oaks and red birches, poplar and chestnut. Mixed in among them are the evergreen trees, magnolia and hemlock, spruce and fir and pine. Here grows the dawn redwood, ancient cousin of the American sequoia and known only as a fossil in the rest of the world.

Under the trees there's a tangled undergrowth of tropical vine and fern, rich green moss, and bamboo thicket. The Chinese call

3: Prologue

the species of bamboo that grows here "arrow bamboo" because the nomads of long ago made their arrows out of it. It is also known as Chinacane. It has slender stems, the largest of which are about an inch and a half in diameter. And it thrives in the moist air and heavy rainfall.

Where the towering trees grow thickly, the bamboos are stunted because they do not get much sunlight. But in large sections of the wilderness, the tree cover is sparser. This started to happen long ago when primeval trees were cut down by nomads who wanted to raise maize to augment their hunting. As the centuries went by, the nomads were joined by lumbermen who also felled the forest cover. Free of shade, the bamboos flourished, forming a wall some ten to twelve feet high, with stems so thickly crowded together that it is almost impossible for human beings to penetrate. Through this jungle meander trails of all sizes, worn there by the creatures who inhabit the area.

Above 12,000 feet, the bamboo thickets and the forest trees die out and rhododendron bushes take over. Higher still, the belt of rhododendron also disappears. At this altitude there are only open alpine meadows broken by barren cliffs and steep rock-strewn slides, or screes, that stretch upward to the snow peaks.

This wilderness with its various belts is the home of many strange and rare creatures. So precious are they to the People's Republic of China that in 1965 it created several wildlife preserves in the area. No human being is allowed to enter the preserves without permission, even to gather medicinal herbs.

One of the sanctuaries is Wanglang Preserve, which lies in the mountainous region of north-central Szechuan Province. The closest village to the preserve is Kao Keng, some 8,000 feet above sea level and less than two miles south of the preserve's border.

In Kao Keng, the dozen or so houses that line both banks of a small stream are built of wood. The families who live in them are Tibetans. To keep warm, even the children wear long woolen robes, or *shubas*, that reach to the calves of their legs. Near the village lie fields of oats, buckwheat, highland barley, and maize, for it is much too cold here to grow rice or even wheat. Beyond the fields are pasture lands where the villagers keep a few cows and sheep. They also have beehives. They augment their income by collecting the medicinal herbs that grow in moist places on the craggy mountain slopes that surround them.

The people of Kao Keng feel a special responsibility toward the wildlife that lives so near them. There are species of pheasants here that cannot be seen wild in any other place in the world. White Tibetan snowcocks live high up on the slopes, near the line of perpetual snow. In the upper brushlands are equally rare Lady Amherst pheasants with great green ruffs and graceful blue-brown plumage. Down in the lower forests gold-and-scarlet golden pheasants hide themselves.

Many of the native animals are equally rare. On the alpine meadows Tibetan blue sheep graze. Takin, serow, and goral, all members of the goat family, frequent rocky slopes, alpine meadows, and forests. The leopard and lynx, the Himalayan black bear, and the Tibetan blue bear roam at will throughout this wilderness. Various species of deer graze in open woodland glades and alpine meadows. The lesser panda with its fiery red coat and the black-and-white giant panda make their home in the bamboo jungles.

The giant panda, rarest of these animals, is the most important to the villagers. They are better acquainted with their strange neighbor than any other persons in the world. They call it the "bear-cat."

5: Prologue

1
Finding Mates .

For most of the year the giant pandas are silent, but twice a year, in the spring and again in the fall, the deep fluting roar of the males can be heard drifting through the bamboo jungles.

It is April in Wanglang Preserve. High in a tall spruce tree one of these males, a nine-year-old, is perched. He is about six feet long from the tip of his nose to the end of his stumpy tail. And he stands about four feet high when he is on all fours. But now he is just a great unwieldy ball of white-and-black fur crouched in a fork of the tree.

His legs are black, and a broad black band crosses his shoulders. His ears are black, too, and large black circles around the eyes give his face a sad clownlike look. His pelt is a woolly coat of stiff springy hair that lies close to his skin in layers, two inches deep in some places. Beneath this outer coat he has another very thick, somewhat oily undercoat. It is enough to keep him warm in the 8,000- to 12,000-foot altitudes where he spends most of his time. Here the temperature seldom goes above 15 degrees in the winter and averages 65 to 70 degrees in August, the hottest summer month. Usually it is damp and chill the year round.

Though this panda ordinarily weighs some three hundred

pounds, he has lost his customary sleek look, for he has eaten next to nothing in the past few days. All his being is concentrated on finding a mate.

For the better part of the year he lives a solitary life, as all pandas do. Only at the mating season do males and females come together. Then giant pandas may be seen in twos and even threes as they search and spar for mates.

There is a tangled underbrush of bamboo around the tree in which the panda is perched, and some scattered open spaces out of which other trees rise. Occasionally the panda stops his roar to scrutinize the wilderness below him. Though he is rather near-sighted, his sense of smell and hearing more than make up for his poor vision.

He knows that if he waits long enough and calls long enough, somewhere in that jungle a female panda will hear him and come his way. The wind will bring him her scent and the sound of her movements through the bamboo, and he will clamber down to join her.

At the very moment the giant panda is roaring in his treetop, a female panda is also starting on her quest. She lumbers along one of the trails. At two hundred pounds she weighs somewhat less than the male, and her ponderous body resembles a great stuffed toy. She walks flat-footed as does a bear. But her stride is longer. Her gait is a kind of pigeon-toed shuffle, and she sways from side to side, her head bent low, her stubby white tail pressed against her body. For several days now, the female has been eating even less than the male. But despite her fasting she is quite energetic, pressing forward doggedly while emitting sheeplike bleats, *he he he.*

Though she is large, she moves like a shadow through bamboo thickets that are difficult for human beings to penetrate. The way

8: Finding Mates

leads upward steeply, skirting narrow ledges, sometimes taking a sudden plunge downward into dark ravines. But the female panda travels with surprising agility.

When she comes to the banks of a chattering, ice-cold stream, she stops to lap at the water, then fords it. She will cross several more small rivers before she reaches her destination.

She isn't carrying out a haphazard search for a mate. This route is familiar to her. For four years, ever since she reached the mating age at six, she has followed it. She knows instinctively that somewhere along it, a male panda will be waiting for her.

This year, as in every other year, she leaves behind signs for any male panda to read. She does this by raising her shoulders, bending her head even lower, and lifting her stubby tail to press her rump against a rocky ledge or a tree trunk. She rubs back and forth, depositing a small patch of glandular moisture. Though the substance is almost odorless to human beings, it gives off a scent that will attract the male to her.

Every now and then the panda stops to listen, her head cocked to one side, her short ears pricked up. From far away comes a low, deep call. When she hears it she always stops to leave another scent, then continues on her way.

Each time the call seems closer. At last it is quite loud. She is approaching the old spruce tree where the male panda is sitting. Her odor drifts up to him, and he grows excited. Quickly he slithers down the tree, rump first. When he is within a few feet of the ground he jumps down and hurries off in the direction of the scent and the bleating.

He is eager to mate, and as he nears the female, he gives a loud roar and starts running toward her. But the female's mating time has not yet come, and no mating can take place until both animals are equally ready.

9:   *Finding Mates*

As the male panda comes closer, the female turns and runs from him. The male chases her and presently overtakes her. Immediately he tries to mate with her, but she backs away in fury. Her great paw strikes out at him. Her long, sharp claws rake across his shoulder drawing blood, leaving behind a jagged flesh wound.

Claw gashes such as this are common among adult male pandas, and many bear the scars of such encounters. But a little thing like a clawing will not stop the male panda. During the days that follow he continues to trail the female, making yodeling calls to her, which she ignores. When he gets too close, she turns and lashes out. Again and again she draws blood, but he will not give up until his mating period has passed. It will be a very short period, usually no more than ten days. If the female panda is not ready before then, the male will be unable to mate this spring. He will have to wait until his capability returns during the fall mating season.

This male panda is not the only one to pick up the scent of the female. Suddenly one morning another roar comes from the bamboo thickets. A second male eager for mating is on the trail.

It is too much for the female. She runs for a tall spruce. Hugging the trunk by pressing the soles of her feet against it, she shimmies up, humping her back like a caterpillar while her claws dig into the bark leaving long gashes. Now and then she snatches at branches and snags from broken limbs to support herself.

At last she reaches a comfortable crotch between the trunk and a high branch. She settles into it, curling up in a snug ball. There, chattering her teeth in excitement, she watches the male panda below her. He is busily stalking about the area, marking rocks and tree trunks with his own scent. Sometimes he stands on his front legs and backs his rump high up the trunk of some tree to leave a scent there too. He wants it understood by every visitor that this is

his territory and the female is to be his mate. If any other male panda enters it, he can expect a fight.

He hasn't finished his marking when a second roar sounds close at hand. Out of the bamboo thickets plods another panda. He sniffs at the scent of the first male, but it doesn't frighten him off. The attraction he feels for the female perched in the spruce tree is too strong for that. He is going to make a challenge.

On he comes. The first male goes to meet him. Swinging their huge paws, they swat at each other with resounding blows. They snap and bite with their great teeth. Back and forth, round and round they go. Finally the second panda begins to back away; soon he slinks off into the bamboo thickets. The victor celebrates his triumph by rolling around on the ground.

Early the next morning the female panda, having reached her mating peak, slithers down the tree. Now it is her turn to do the chasing. But she does it backward, presenting her rump to the male panda. As she comes toward him, he backs away to the tree, where he sits down propped against it. When the female reaches him he clasps her around the waist and holds her tightly, giving a loud cry. And so they mate.

The actual mating lasts only a couple of minutes. When it is over the female panda turns on the male, tired of his company. She gives him a hard bite that warns him to be on his way. He scrambles to his feet and ambles off. The tie of nature that has drawn them so closely together for a brief spell is broken.

No sooner has he disappeared than the female forgets about him. She is very tired; the activities of the mating season along with her long fast have worn her out. Sluggishly she makes herself a nest in the bamboo underbrush at the foot of the tree, turning round and round until she has formed a circular bed of crushed bamboo stalks. On these she stretches out, flat on her back. In no time she is fast asleep.

12: Finding Mates

2
Wanderer

LATE in the afternoon the female giant panda wakens in the cool green shadows under the tree. She stretches once, then slowly staggers to her feet. From somewhere in the distance the fluting roar of a male panda comes to her ears. But she no longer responds. She feels only a faint stir of hunger. Wandering into the bamboo thickets, she searches out some tender bamboo shoots and begins to nibble on them. At present only a few bites will satisfy her. But in the weeks to come, her appetite will quickly return. A month from now she will be eating more than ever, for she is carrying new life within her.

Like the bear, the giant panda is classified as a carnivore, or flesh eater, because it will occasionally devour small animals or birds. But its main diet is made up of plant life, principally the leaves, shoots, and stems of the arrow bamboo. Except for its tender shoots, bamboo is so tough that only an animal especially equipped to handle it could survive on this diet. The panda is such an animal. Over centuries it has developed a massive head with strong jaw muscles and huge teeth, the upper surfaces of which are deeply ridged.

With these great teeth the panda bites off a bamboo stem close to the ground. She picks it up with her handlike front paw, which appears to have six digits rather than five. Actually the sixth claw is only an elongated part of her wristbone covered by a tough pad of flesh, which acts like a thumb. It is muscular and supple so that she can easily handle even the slenderest stalk.

She lifts the stalk to her mouth and strips off the tough outer sheath with a sideways jerk of her head and a twist of her paws in the opposite direction. Then she places the stalk lengthwise between her cheek teeth and bites off a chunk. Slowly and methodically she chews on it with those great grinding molars.

But even massive molars cannot do a thorough job on the tough bamboo, and the panda swallows bits and fragments whole. The sharp bamboo slivers proceed down her esophagus without harming it because it has a horny lining. Her stomach walls, too, are thick and muscular, resembling a chicken gizzard. But the intestines, which should have been long enough to digest the bamboo, are instead very short, only about five and a half times the length of the panda's body. This is short even for a carnivore, and much too short for an animal whose main diet is green stuff. No one can explain why the panda's intestines did not develop as did its jaws and teeth, esophagus and stomach. But because they are so short, much of the nutrition in the stalks passes out of the panda's body. One of the most obvious signs of a panda's presence are numerous large droppings that contain quantities of undigested bamboo.

To sustain herself, the giant panda has to spend as much as twelve hours a day eating. Her intake may be as high as twenty pounds of bamboo daily. Sometimes she stays in one spot long enough to gnaw off all the bamboos in an area some sixteen feet square; at other times she eats on the move.

After feeding, the panda places her front paws before her face

14: Wanderer

and licks them clean, going over her forearms too, and finally wiping one paw over her face as a cat does. If a bamboo sliver sticks between her teeth, she uses the claws of one of her front paws to pick it out. Occasionally, perhaps to sharpen her claws, she strips away the bark from the entire lower trunk of a tree, up to a height of several feet.

The panda has no set schedule, though she sleeps more at noonday and midnight than at other times. She rests when the mood is on her and in almost any position you could name— sitting up with her back against a tree, lying flat on her back with her legs in the air, or curled up in a ball. She spends a great deal of time, too, just twisting and rolling on the ground for exercise, scratching herself and licking her fur. For all her size she can twist herself into so many strange postures that she looks like a rubber animal.

Sometimes she stands up on her hind legs like a bear, especially when she wants to reach for something. All pandas do this. But nobody has ever seen one take a single step in that position. Perhaps this is because the panda's bones are heavier than those of the bear, which sometimes does walk upright. The added weight may be too much to support on the panda's hind legs alone.

One of the panda's favorite positions is to sit with her back against a tree, one hind leg lifted straight up in the air. With her chin propped on her raised foot she sits staring off into space. Occasionally when she's dreaming away like this she is interrupted by a swarm of tiny brown birds whose territory she has ignorantly invaded. Scolding and chattering and fluttering around her angrily, they finally drive her away to find a quieter retreat.

Everywhere the birds are sensitive to intrusion this time of year, for it is spring and their mating season too. Their cries and

15: Wanderer

Peking robins

songs assault the panda's ears. All night long the *huuuh uh huuh*, of the great tawny owl can be heard as he howls out his welcome to the season. But when he is courting he adds an embellishment, a quick trill with an *oo. Kyuwitt, kyuwitt,* his mate replies.

Other birds are also giving voice to the usually quiet wilderness. Yellow-eyed flycatchers and gregarious bubuls in scarlet topknots call to their mates at intervals. The little Szechuan cuckoo's strange cry floats through the woodlands day and night. Most melodious of all is the song of the black, red, and gold Peking robin, the Chinese nightingale with his clear sweet melody; his *tee tee tee tee* floats out from the spruce and pine forests which are his home. Sometimes the panda can even hear the loud melodious whistles of the mating Tibetan snowcocks drifting down the mountainside from as far as a mile away.

Once in a while a shy russet-colored civet darts in front of the panda in pursuit of a centipede. The civet, cousin to the mongoose, looks something like a cat but with protruding eyes, shorter legs, and a longer muzzle.

Occasionally the panda's path crosses those of the Himalayan black bears, "dog bears," as the villagers call them, with their pointed snoots and the broad white crescents on their chests. The black bears, usually solitary like the panda, are now seeking mates, as are the rarer Tibetan blue bears, which the villagers call "horse bears." They are larger than the black bear or the panda and have pale straw-colored coats. They are very aggressive, and their mating period is a fearsome thing.

Seen together, bears and giant pandas look as if they might be related species, though the giant panda has a much larger and rounder head than the bear. The skeletons of both animals, the arrangement of their muscles and the shape of their brains, are

17: Wanderer

similar. Both species have short and stubby tails and both shimmy up trees and descend them rump first.

Now and then at dusk the giant panda meets another possible relative, the lesser panda, wandering through the wilderness. Unlike the giant panda, the lesser panda is a sociable fellow. He usually chooses one mate and lives with her for life. Together they raise a litter of cubs every year in the hollow of some old tree.

The lesser panda is only about two feet long, with a bushy ringed tail that adds another eighteen inches to its length. It is clothed in shining chestnut-red woolly fur that gleams in the twilight. The black markings about its face and ears, the white spots over each eye and on the tips of its ears, give it a pixieish expression.

Like the giant panda, the lesser panda feeds mostly on bamboo. It, too, is equipped with powerful jaws, huge teeth, and handlike front paws, though it doesn't have a sixth claw. It also has very short intestines. These are some of the reasons many zoologists place the giant panda with the lesser panda in the raccoon family. Others maintain that the giant panda and the lesser panda are not related but only developed in a similar fashion because their ancestors both took to eating bamboo.

Besides bamboo, the lesser panda eats fruit buds, leaves, insects, and larvae and is not above robbing birds' nests of eggs. It doesn't much care for meat, but it will occasionally grab up a mouse as it skitters across a clearing.

Usually the lesser panda spends the day in sleep, curled up like a dog or cat on the branch of a tree with its tail over its head, or with its head tucked under its chest and between its forelegs. When a male lesser panda talks with his mate it is in a series of short whistles or squeaking notes. Occasionally he emits a loud *wha wha wha,* sounding so much like a small child crying for its

18: Wanderer

mother that among the villagers he's earned the name, "child of the mountains."

Traveling through the open clearings, the giant panda often catches the sounds of timid creatures warning their neighbors of the presence of nearby danger from their natural enemies, such as the wild dog or the leopard. At the warning sneeze of the leader, a pack of tawny musk deer skitter off for safety with rumps and heads strained high, half galloping, half jumping along with all four feet off the ground.

The doglike yaps of the shy muntjac, or barking deer, signal its fellows to disappear into the bamboo thickets, where it is almost impossible for a leopard to spring. The panda may also hear the warning cry of the dark woolly sambar, an antlered deer, whose loud whistle sends the herd off with flashing heels and a flicking of tails revealing white undersides.

When the panda senses danger herself, she has two choices. She can melt into the thickets or shimmy up a tall tree where she crouches on a high fork. Here, hiding among the thick leaves, she clicks her teeth together in a chittering warning that sounds like twigs being rubbed together in a wind.

Treetops are one of the panda's favorite resting places anyway. Here she is safe from prowling leopards and packs of wild dogs that are as rapacious as wolves. From her high perch she can look down dreamily on a silent world. Long, pale green-gray streamers of moss festoon the tall spruce trees and sway in the wind. Beyond the clearing, bamboo thickets stretch away on all sides, rising in green phalanxes toward the distant snowy peaks.

In the open space below the panda's perch, a rust-colored lynx, a little larger than an oversize cat, steals across the bed of soft moss and springs on two green monal pheasants engaged in their courting dance. Just in time the birds scatter into the brush,

The snow leopard

piping loudly. Of as much danger to them is the great eagle soaring overhead. The eagle is a carnivore with hungry eaglets to feed and no bird, vole, pika, or meadow mouse is safe from it; nor are fawns or the kids of the mountain goats, blue sheep lambs, or

21: Wanderer

the piglets of the wild boar. With its sharp talons and tearing beak, the eagle can overpower creatures far larger than itself.

Certainly the eagle would have no problem with a newborn cub of the giant panda. But the adult panda need have no fear of eagles. She is too big and strong to be troubled with many enemies. Bears offer her no real threat. Though she may spat briefly with them over territory, she usually avoids them. Shaggy wild dogs that roam the wilderness and look much like German shepherds with their plumed tails and lean faces are much smaller than she. But a pack of them could be dangerous if they managed to corner her.

Another threat is the snow leopard. This handsome cat, found only in the Himalayan, Tibetan, and Altai mountain ranges of Asia, is easily the most beautiful cat in the world. Some four feet long, it has a tail almost the same length, and for most of the year it wears a creamy coat of thick fur decorated with dark rosettes. It roams the mountain slopes above 8,000 feet, seldom dropping below that altitude. It follows the life of a hunter, preying on any creature that it can surprise and kill, from wild sheep to goats and deer. Snow leopard young are born in the summer; to keep them fed the adult leopard becomes very bold indeed.

Face to face with the giant panda, the snow leopard would be no match. A loud bark from the panda, a swipe with one massive paw, and a ferocious snap of the great jaws would easily drive off the leopard. But the big cat hunts by stealth and depends on a sudden spring and a well-aimed strike at a vulnerable spot. The panda cannot rely on her poor eyesight to warn her of danger, but has to depend on her acute senses of smell and hearing to alert her to this sly enemy which, when famished, will take any chance.

3
Alpine Meadows

THROUGH the quiet wilderness the giant panda moves like a great black-and-white shadow. The dense bamboo thickets mounting up almost perpendicular mountain slopes rustle with every breath of wind. As she plods along, dust from dead leaves blows into her eyes; every now and again she must stop to rub at them with a paw.

Though she seems to be wandering aimlessly about, she is actually following a meandering course that will eventually lead upward. As summer comes, the lower forests are too hot for her. At 70 degrees, especially if it is humid too, she becomes listless. If the temperature rises higher than this, she pants and her pulse races. She loses energy and appetite. If she were to stay in the heat, she would sicken and die.

Summer brings the rainy season, and winter's snow disappears into muddy slush. Frequent downpours send torrents streaming through the jungles. The whole world seems to split apart as huge avalanches of mud, boulders, and tremendous rocks thunder down to the valleys, destroying everything in their path. But the giant panda is used to these violent outbursts and continues on her way undisturbed.

Sometimes, instead of rain, chill mists and fogs drench the bamboos, showering the panda with drops of moisture as she passes through. Underfoot, thick green moss forms a deceptive coverlet over everything, concealing decaying tree trunks, beds of rotten bamboo stalks, sharply tilted slabs of rock, and other pitfalls. Moisture and occasional ice make the moss slippery. But the panda moves easily over the glassy surfaces, even up the steepest slopes. Hair growing on the soles of her feet gives her traction, and her claws help her to keep her footing.

As she mounts the higher slopes the wind becomes very chill, sometimes bringing snowfalls with it. The panda rejoices in the cold white powder under the trees. She rolls about in it and presses handfuls of it against her face before continuing onward.

All around her, the small creatures that live in rock clefts or underground burrows or hollow trees are still conducting their mating rituals. The young of the shrew are easy game for the panda, as are meadow mice and the long-tailed harvest mice and slate gray field rats. So is the pika, which looks like a tiny rabbit with short, rounded ears. As the pikas work gathering greens for the winter, their short bleats sound over the mountain slopes, signaling to one another, perhaps warning of danger. At the first hint of danger they'll pop out of sight into burrows or rock crevices. But occasionally one of them is careless—a sad mistake when the giant panda is around. Out darts a huge paw, breaking a bleat midway through, and a tiny pika disappears into the great jaws. It will have no use for its summer harvest now.

As the panda pushes forward through a woodland glade, life explodes above her with a burst of chattering voices, welcoming, mocking, scolding. Large brown eyes follow her movements with a glittering stare from their high tree perch. These are the rare golden monkeys, whose beautiful thick fur ranges from snow white in the babies to a pale gold in the females and rich russet bronze tones in the males. Bright blue, turquoise, or violet patterns spread across their upturned noses, like butterflies perched there with outstretched wings.

In their thick coats, the golden monkeys, like the pandas, are unable to stand the summer heat. Now this company of eighty or so is headed for the upper regions and has stopped along the way to feed. They nibble on tender leaves, ripening berries, insects, and eggs, and their trail is strewn with empty acorn shells. Their appetite satisfied for the moment, the monkeys continue on their journey, flying and swinging through the treetops. The giant panda is alone again.

Her trail leads along the margin of a steep slope that falls away to a rushing torrent some five hundred feet below. Suddenly she hears the *clomp clomp clomp* of hooves behind her. The mighty takin that has been wintering in the valleys is migrating upward too.

The takin is a strange animal found nowhere else in the world. Some scientists place it with the musk ox, which is a cross between an antelope and a goat. Measuring from the shoulder, the takin is more than four feet high and weighs up to seven hundred pounds. Its short sturdy legs and feet are goatlike, but with huge hooves often six inches in diameter. It has a long face with a humped nose and a broad muzzle, and its head is crowned with curved horns. Its coat is dense and shaggy.

During the spring the takins have been grazing in the valleys. But with the approaching summer they begin gathering at the natural salt licks on the lower mountain slopes. Over the years

25: Alpine Meadows

the takins have beaten well-worn trails to these licks. By June, large herds are milling around them.

The herds split up into companies of a hundred or so, each with its own old bull leader. The companies set off along the wide trails that lead to the alpine meadows. Despite their size—they are almost two and a half times heavier than the panda—and clumsy appearance, takins are surprisingly agile. When frightened or enraged they will thunder down on the offender with flashing hooves and lowered heads, so swiftly that it's difficult to get out of their way.

Now, one after the other, the great creatures come up the trail toward the panda. She knows better than to confront them and chooses the simplest course out of her predicament. Up go her front paws to cover her eyes, and over she rolls into a great furry ball. The "ball" gives a bounce, and over the edge of the steep slope tumbles the panda. Down she goes without taking so much as a peek around her. When she reaches the margin of the stream, ice-cold spray showers her. Only then does she uncoil, shaking herself.

A large gray water shrew mole, startled by the racket, pokes his head out of his burrow to take a look. But the panda ignores him. She is very thirsty, and the water is refreshingly sweet. After drinking her fill she wades into the torrent and easily swims across it, stopping at the far shallows to scoop up a small fish and pop it into her mouth. Then she is on her way again, plodding up the steep bamboo-clothed opposite slope.

Day after day she travels in this leisurely fashion. Each slope she climbs brings her higher into the mountains. Almost every jagged ravine she crosses is filled with a torrent of whitish green water. Presently she emerges from the dense bamboo jungle into

The takin

more open thickets under a tree cover of towering spruce and lichen-patterned alders.

Here the panda sometimes meets up with the oddly fashioned serow, a member of the goat family found only in Asia. Brownish black, with horns close to ten inches long, the serow sports a beard from the corners of its mouth to the base of its huge ears, giving it a whimsical, melancholy expression.

The serow prefers to live in thick spruce forests, and it stays in practically the same territory year round. On the other hand, its smaller cousin, the goral, occasionally crosses the panda's route while roaming across the rocky screes. The goral, which also lives only in Asia, is a graceful olive-buff animal about the size of a goat. Its most amazing feature are its hooves, which have shallow depressions that act like suction cups. The main digits and dewclaws also end in black rounded rubberlike soles, which enable it to keep a firm footing on sloping rocks. With these the goral can bounce easily along on ledges that are so narrow even a rabbit would have difficulty perching on them.

Beyond the bamboo thickets the panda enters the belt of low rhododendron trees and bushes that in late May and early June blaze with multicolored blossoms—reds and pinks, whites and yellows. Rhododendrons are evergreens, but because the ice and snow linger so long in these regions, their leaves are warped and curl up in tubelike shapes.

Still higher she climbs until the belt of rhododendron also dwindles away. Now there are only open alpine meadows broken by barren cliffs; steep rock-strewn slides stretch upward to the perpetual snowpeaks, gleaming like crystal against the clear blue sky. Summer warmth strews the rich meadow grass with large red, blue, and golden mountain poppies, primulas, and tiny blue lilies. But even summer weather is uncertain. In late July and early August, the hottest season, the temperature averages only 50 degrees. A sudden blizzard may sweep down over the meadows and bury the green grass and flowers. When that happens, only a few tiny lilies or golden poppies encased in ice remain to remind the frozen world that spring has really come.

This is the home of the wild blue sheep, the bharal, that live at 12,000- to 17,000-foot elevations. They are neither sheep nor goats but spring from a common ancestor that existed in the Early Pliocene era in China. Their faces are long, their eyes large. Small pointed ears and curving horns sprout from their heads. Clothed in grayish blue hair, they can stand motionless among the rocks, hidden from enemies by their natural coloration.

The blue sheep share the meadowlands with the rare Thorald's deer who carry great branching antlers on their heads. Both blue sheep and deer have sentries to warn them of danger. But they ignore the panda venturing into their meadows, as she ignores them. She is attracted to the wealth of succulent plants that the summer sun has brought up. Along the banks of the streams that course through the meadowlands grow gentians, irises, crocuses, Chinese vines, and tufted grasses. The panda grubs them up and devours them in quantity—they are a change from her common diet of bamboo and occasional rodents. But she is uneasy in these open lands where the cunning leopard roams at will, so she never strays far from the tree cover.

By late August, the period that the Chinese call the Time of Cessation of Heat, night frosts begin to shrivel plants and grasses. Snowstorms become more frequent and fiercer, ruffling the thick fleece of the blue sheep.

The giant panda turns back into familiar territory, the sanctu-

29: Alpine Meadows

ary of the bamboo thickets. Her swelling abdomen is plainly visible now. She is normally so round and large that if she were going to have just one cub it wouldn't be obvious, but the size of her abdomen indicates she will be bearing twins or even triplets, though triplets are rare among pandas.

Her breasts—she has four of them, one pair on her chest, another on her abdomen—are swelling too. Her appetite is gradually falling off; all she craves are bamboo stalks. But as the days go by she eats fewer and fewer of these. She knows from the growing weight within her that her cubs are about to be born. She must select a good den in which to give birth.

The black bears and the Tibetan blue bears also are looking for dens in which they can hibernate for the winter. They are sleek from their summer of stuffing in preparation for their long winter's sleep. The pregnant females will waken to give birth to their young during this hibernation period; then, with their babies safely suckling, they will return to their half-sleep again. When they emerge the following spring they will be accompanied by their cubs.

The giant panda does not hibernate, but the female must hole up for a while during the birth and the early weeks of her cubs' existence. For this she needs a place that is both comfortable and snug.

At last, on a steep slope covered thickly with bamboo, she comes upon a kind of cave formed by an overhanging rock. Old droppings around the cave show that it has been used often before. It is this panda's special birthing place to which she has returned year after year. The cave is satisfactory in every way. It is roomy and well concealed. The bamboo thickets that grow around it will provide her with food, and a small stream sparkling in a nearby gully will satisfy her thirst.

30: Alpine Meadows

The blue sheep

But neither food nor drink interest the panda at present. Now she has stopped eating altogether. She seems to have lost most of her energy too, as she languidly moves about preparing things. She cuts down bamboo stalks and drags them into the cave to form a nest. When she has finished she spends most of her time sitting in her den or sprawled outside resting. For long periods she lies in a heavy sleep—waiting, waiting.

4
The Cubs Are Born

THE DAY of birth finally arrives. The panda knows her time has come and crouches in her nest, feeling her belly moving up and down in heavy rhythmic movements. It contracts and relaxes, contracts and relaxes, as though it were being squeezed at intervals by a gigantic invisible hand. At first the contractions are few and far apart, but as time goes by they increase in number and intensity. The giant panda helps the process by pushing down with her abdominal muscles.

Suddenly a cub is born. Head first, it drops to the ground, a squirming grublike creature weighing only four or five ounces, no bigger than a small rat. It is difficult to believe that it will ever reach the size of its two-hundred-pound mother.

Its eyes are tightly shut, and it is toothless. Its body, which has a sparse sprinkling of short white baby hair, is a light pink color. Its tail is about one-third its body length, and its head is rounder and blunter than its mother's. It is a male, though it is impossible now to judge its sex. Even after it has matured at six years of age it will be difficult to see its genitalia because, as in all pandas, male or female, they will be concealed in protective layers of fat.

Only at the mating season do the male sex organs protrude from that fleshy pocket and become plainly visible.

Now the tiny creature squirms on the ground helplessly. Twenty minutes after its arrival a second cub, a female, is born. Her sex is no more apparent than that of her brother.

The exertion has worn out the mother. She is panting hard, her breath coming in short, uneven gasps. Even though there is nothing in her stomach she begins heaving with nausea. She is very weak, but she props herself up in a sitting position and tenderly picks up the tiny cubs one at a time with her mouth and enfolds them in her arms.

The little creatures are covered with a sticky birth substance, and she starts licking them clean. She licks for two hours before she is satisfied. Then she raises them to her nipples, and they settle down to nurse. The mother panda falls asleep with the cubs suckling at her breasts.

Outside the dark cave world of the panda, autumn is taking possession of the mountains. Frost touches birches, poplars, and chestnut trees, and they burst into colors of bronze and gold and flame. Those creatures of the wild who are stirred by fall mating instincts begin their courtship games.

Male musk deer, usually timid, meet each other in fierce challenge. Entwining their necks around each other to get a good hold, they gash into hide and muscle with their rapier-sharp tusks. The fights are so fierce that before the season is over all the males will bear new scars to join the crisscross of old ones.

The red deer that live in the wooded valley bottoms, the gorals, and the blue sheep are also dueling for their right to mate. Wild male boars, who have been living alone, grubbing and eating their way through the forest, forget about food and the pleasures of a solitary life and begin trekking for the mating places. Here the huge boars fight one another with their venomous tusks until they have won their females. Then round and round in a circle the male drives the female, boxing her roughly with his snout and emitting loud rhythmic grunts.

Out in the forests the lesser panda is also courting, but in a gentler style. Its *wha wha wha* floats through the forest and is joined by the mating call of the giant panda. Sunk in a deep sleep, the female panda does not even hear it.

For a day after the birth of the twins, the giant panda continues to rest and sleep in her den, hugging her cubs to her. When they are hungry they cry out like babies or yap like young puppies, their voices astonishingly loud for such tiny creatures. Then their mother wakens and with paws and mouth gently guides the little mouths to her nipples. When they settle down to nurse she falls asleep again, only to be awakened an hour or two later. In the weeks ahead, the cubs will nurse six to twelve times every twenty-four hours.

The constant feeding has its effect; as the days go by, the cubs start filling out and losing their ratlike appearance. About a week after their birth the hair on their ears and around their eyes and shoulders starts turning gray. The grayish color soon spreads to their front limbs and darkens on their ears and around their eyes. Within two weeks their hind limbs as well as their front ones have turned black, and the black rings around their eyes have grown larger. Though their eyes are still shut, the rings make it look as if the tiny creatures are wearing black spectacles that give them a roguish expression.

By the sixteenth day their chests start turning black, and the black circles around the eyes change into long, slanting splotches like those of their mother. In the next few days the neck, front, and back have turned black. Within three weeks the color has spread over the whole neck and chest, while the white hair has grown longer. Now they look like miniatures of their mother except for their rather long tails and the lighter color of their black markings. They won't turn a deep ebony until the fiftieth day.

During their first month the cubs' eyes have remained closed; they have no reaction at all to light, even when sunbeams slant into the den striking against their closed lids. Only by the end of that first month do they start showing sensitivity by wrinkling up their eyes when the light falls on them.

One day, the male cub manages to open an eye halfway for an instant. The light is too much and down blinks the lid. Immediately he opens the other eye, also halfway and just for an instant. It will be two weeks before he will be able to keep both eyes open at once.

Ten days later, his sister's eyes are fully open too. But even though both cubs' eyes are now open, their vision is still so poor that everything is a blur. The blur will clear away gradually in the weeks ahead, and by the time they are three months old they will be able to see more plainly.

In the beginning, however, they don't have much use for eyes. They spend most of their time sleeping and nursing. Their muscles are so weak that, try as they might, they can't pull themselves up to their mother's nipples but sway from side to side, whimpering. Their mother sits down when one or the other of them cries out like this. With her front paws she picks up the hungry cub and places it gently on her stomach. From there it crawls to one of her nipples and begins suckling, sprawled out like a human baby.

As the weeks go by the male cub begins to outstrip his sister in size and strength. Even at birth he was bigger and stronger. He is also more assertive. He cries the loudest, catching their mother's attention first. Only after she has helped him to his feeding does she realize the second cub is whimpering too. By the time the smaller cub starts nursing, the larger one has already greedily gulped down a good share of his milk. When he finishes all of it, he shoves away his weaker sister to get at her share too.

This is what usually happens when a panda has twins. The stronger of the two attracts more attention, while the weaker one is unintentionally neglected and often dies as a result. Instead of fighting back, the little female cub just whimpers a little and falls asleep only half full. All this shows up in the weight of the pandas at the end of the first month. The male cub weighs four pounds, the female only three.

Life isn't just nursing and sleeping for the panda family in their den. The mother panda likes to have some fun with her cubs. She nuzzles them affectionately and sometimes hugs them tightly to her breast. When they become impatient and begin to wriggle, she calms them down by stroking their furry little bodies with her big paw. As they grow bigger she plays a little game with them. Back and forth, back and forth she gently tosses them, one at a time, from one arm to the other, almost like a human mother rocking her babies.

During the month following her cubs' birth, the giant panda ate very little. But as the young pandas' appetites grow, their mother has to provide them with greater and greater quantities of milk, and she begins to feed voraciously. Soon she is taking more than one and a half times her normal amount of food, still mainly bamboo.

When she goes out to feed she takes her cubs with her, carrying one in her mouth and hobbling along on three legs with the other cub clutched in her fourth paw. She eats sitting or lying down with the cubs resting on her belly.

Beyond the gloomy den lies a strange and delightful world,

38: The Cubs Are Born

dressed in the sparkling icicles of late fall. Glittering ice coats every hair on every leaf in the bamboo thickets. When the mother goes to drink she finds a thin sheath of ice over the little stream. She has to break through it with a massive hind foot to get at the water underneath. When, after drinking her fill, she turns back to the bamboo thickets, the icicles that have formed in the thick fur of her foot chink and chitter until they melt in the sun.

By the time the cubs are two months old they stop suckling at night, though their mother's milk is still their only food. They no longer cry like babies or yap like puppies when they're hungry. The larger they grow, the softer their voices become, so that presently the only sound they make to get attention is a low, bleating *e-e.*

Within two and a half months they are able to put weight on their hind legs and even take a couple of steps. By the third month the largest cub, who now weighs more than eleven pounds, can walk almost four feet at a time before toppling over. His smaller sister, who weighs only nine pounds, can scarcely go three feet without falling.

Now that they are bigger, their mother likes to romp with them occasionally in the soft snow drifts, batting them lightly with her great paws and rolling them over and over like balls. She always ends the game by hugging them to her and letting them nurse.

The cubs like to tumble about with each other, too. But most of all they enjoy playing the toboggan game on their mother's back. While she is eating they haul themselves over her haunches and up onto her shoulders. It is a long distance for their weak-muscled arms. They use their sharp claws to clutch at her fur for support. When their strength gives out they just hang there, catching their breaths and resting against the soft springy pelt. Finally they reach the top; they let go and come rolling down. They clamber up again and roll down again, over and over. It's more than fun. It's good safe exercise for their muscles.

These are dangerous times for all the smaller wilderness creatures because predators, gaunt from the winter's scarcity, are wandering the land. Their footprints are visible everywhere. Those of the lynx are small and set close together. There's a longer stride to those of the snow leopard. And there are the jumbled tracks of the wild dogs which, though now an uncommon sight in the preserve, are still around. Overhead is the eagle, a silent predator whose black silhouette can be seen soaring against the wintry sky, ready to swoop down on any small defenseless creature in the open.

And finally there is winter itself, spreading a soft white deceptive blanket over everything. Snow bridges formed across deep chasms give way without warning when the sun comes out. Sudden avalanches tumble down steep slopes with a roar and a crash. There are deep pitfalls everywhere.

It is no place for the inexperienced cubs to go wandering around alone. Safety for them lies either near their mother or in the den which she can easily guard. But now, as they grow older, they begin to stray from her. The male cub takes the lead, the female bumbles along behind.

The mother panda has to round them up continually. Sometimes in her concern she carries them back to the den and sets them down inside. But it doesn't do much good. The white wilderness is too fascinating a place to ignore, and as soon as her back is turned, out they pop again. Back and forth, back and forth, like disobedient human children. They never give up trying to outlast their mother's patience—and they never succeed.

40: The Cubs Are Born

5
Wilderness Tragedy

BY THE TIME the panda cubs are four months old, they can easily mount their mother's back. There, clinging to her fur, they ride safe above the pitfalls of the path below. This is fortunate because with the passage of weeks the swath of bamboo stumps around the den has been steadily growing wider. The giant panda has to travel farther and farther afield for her fare.

With every yard she puts between herself and the den the job of protecting the cubs becomes more difficult for her. She can no longer shoo them into the cave in times of danger. Instead she has to rely on the scattered spruce trees that dot the bamboo thickets. If danger threatens, she will muster the cubs on her back and shimmy up a tree.

At least she no longer has to fear the panda's worst predator—man—who at one time almost exterminated her kind. Man was such a recent enemy the panda had no experience in defending herself against him. For many years the tribes among whom the panda lived never bothered the animal unless it entered their village compounds to rob their beehives. Even then they only drove it away.

To the villagers, the panda was a semi-divinity with its black-and-white human-appearing face and its dexterous front paws. There was a magical quality, too, in the way it moved through the forests like a shadow, despite its huge size. And since, unlike the ferocious bears, it behaved peaceably toward humans, they felt affection for it.

All this changed about a hundred years ago when foreign hunters first began coming to the Szechuan highlands to hunt the panda. At the same time guns were introduced to the area, and high sums were offered for the animal. The impoverished tribespeople, tempted by the money, began to overcome their qualms about killing the panda. They hunted it themselves and also helped Westerners track it through the wilderness.

Using the village hunting dogs to pick up the panda's scent, they would trail the panda. The panda reacted as it did when the wild dogs chased it. It simply shimmied up the nearest tree. Of course it could not know that its only chance of escape was not to let the dogs tree it, but to flee into the bamboo thickets that would hinder the pursuers. Instead, even when it was on the ground it saw so little danger in men that it would walk fearlessly toward them, letting them shoot it at point-blank range.

The People's Republic of China no longer allows man to hunt the panda indiscriminately. Once again, the animal's chief enemies are the wild dogs. Banded together in small packs under a leader, these fearsome predators close in on their kill, their short, shrill yaps ringing a dirge through the wilderness.

When the dogs are running, moles and shrews and pikas pop back into their burrows or crevices. Deer and chamois and blue sheep stand motionless, invisible against the rocky screes. But if the wind carries their scent to the enemy, betraying their presence, they are off in a flash of galloping heels and tossing heads.

The larger more powerful animals, the takins, bears, and pandas, when cornered fight with formidable horns, or with strong muscular arms and tearing teeth. Even the plucky little goral can put up a courageous defense. Its back against a rocky buttress, it will turn on the vicious pack and with its sharp horns will gore any careless animal coming too close.

As the panda and her cubs have begun to venture farther and farther away from the birthing cave, the mother has been constantly on the lookout for wild dogs, for she knows that her best defense is an early warning, which will give her time to flee to safety. The weather has been growing steadily bleaker; with the bitter cold the danger from hungry predators increases, for most game is driven back into shelter and out of reach.

On one crisp morning, alert as usual, the mother starts toward the thickets, carrying her cubs on her back. Snow flurries drifting down from the leaden sky dust the pelts of all three pandas. The wind ruffling their fur has a sharp edge. The whole gray-and-white world seems hushed.

Suddenly the mother panda's ears prick up. The sound of yapping fills the quiet day. In alarm, she streaks for the nearest spruce tree. With the cubs still clinging to her back, she clasps the trunk with both arms and starts to shimmy up the tree.

But she is already too late. Some eight dogs, the largest leading the pack, burst into the clearing. Their jaws are gaping, baring two rows of sharp teeth.

The panda realizes she can never get up the tree in time to escape those rending jaws. So she slides down again, the two cubs

43: Wilderness Tragedy

on her back squealing with terror. She whirls, setting her rump against the trunk. Moving with lightning speed, she reaches out with one strong paw and grabs the leg of the leader as it springs sideways toward the cubs. At the same time she pulls the struggling animal toward her. She opens her powerful jaws and seizes the dog's head. With a loud snap she brings her jaws together and the great molars shatter the animal's skull. The other dogs continue to foam around their quarry. The panda's huge clawed paws keep striking out at them. Her deadly teeth chomp. Another dog, scarcely more than a pup, staggers off dripping with blood.

Suddenly the smaller of the two cubs loses its grip and slips from its mother's back. Before she can retrieve it, or even realize what is happening, one of the dogs darts up, seizes it, and retreats. The rest quickly surround him. Soon they are all fighting over the small broken body.

While the dog pack is distracted, the mother panda quickly shimmies up the tree with the other cub still clinging to her back. From a high fork she looks down at the dogs. They have made short work of her cub. Then, still starved, they turn on their own dead and injured comrades. Quarreling and snarling among themselves, they begin ripping the gaunt winter-famished bodies apart, baring their teeth over the raw steaming flesh. Soon it is all devoured. But there was so little meat on the bones that the dogs are only partially satiated. Roused by their kill and by the taste of blood, they rush to the spruce and begin circling its trunk, springing up at the treed panda and yapping shrilly.

On the limb the mother panda paces to and fro in agitation. The dogs, jumping high in the air, are snapping just below her feet. If one or another were to leap a little higher it might be able to drag her off her perch. With the cub still clinging to her back, she again begins to climb—up, up, stopping only when the branches become

too fragile to bear her weight. *Hu hu hu,* her melancholy cry ripples out over the wilderness as she clings swaying to her lofty perch.

The dogs presently realize their vigil is useless. They break away, disappearing as rapidly as they came. Their yapping fades into the distance.

The panda waits a little longer. Then she slides down the tree, finally dropping to earth. She is panting from exertion. Retrieving the cub from her back, she clasps it tightly to her breast with one paw. On her other three she hobbles across the snow, now littered with black-and-white scraps of panda fur mixed with bits of tawny hair and bones. Everywhere there is a crisscross of sharp footprints, and scattered among them some bloodstains.

For a few seconds the panda stands bewildered above the blood-drenched panda fur. Then she bends her head and sniffs at it. The odor confirms her loss. She sits down and begins to rock back and forth, giving that familiar melancholy wail, *hu hu hu hu.*

Oblivious to the recent tragedy, the cub in her arms whimpers, *eh eh eh,* and struggles to reach for a nipple. Soon it is suckling. But the mother continues to rock back and forth, wailing. It is as though, despite the evidence of her senses, she is calling to her lost cub to return.

As she wails a steady snowfall blurs all under a soft white coverlet that will presently hide every trace of the tragedy. Overhead the wind is whistling loudly now. Twigs rattle. All around, pine trees and bamboo thickets shed their weights of snow with soft plopping sounds.

The cub finishes nursing and lets the nipple fall. With her mouth the mother gently picks up the sleeping baby by the nape of the neck and heads again for the bamboo thickets, the craving in her belly urging her on. It seems as she plods forward that she has already forgotten both the tragedy and her lost cub. But only because her cub is out of sight is it out of mind. If it were miraculously to appear again, even as long as a month later, she would still recognize it. She would welcome it joyfully with open arms, nuzzling it affectionately and clasping it to her breast for nursing. But, for now, she cannot neglect her own needs and those of her remaining cub if they are to stay alive in this harsh world.

6
The Downward Trek

ON THE high slope where the mother panda and her cubs have been living, the snows of early January shawl the bamboo thickets with a heavy crust, making it more and more difficult to get at the plants below. After one night of freezing temperatures, the mother panda finds the stream has become a pale white ribbon of ice. She stamps at it with her heavy hind foot. But this time she cannot break through. The stream is frozen solid. It is time for her and the cub to descend to lower altitudes since she must find free-flowing water to quench her thirst. Ice and snow alone cannot satisfy her.

She leaves behind signs of her long occupancy. A wide area of bamboo stumps surrounds the den. When spring returns, hundreds of new bamboo shoots will sprout up to hide the havoc she has caused, but other marks will remain. The lower trunks of the trees in the vicinity are all scored with her sharp claws, and some have been stripped of their bark. Most of her massive droppings are buried now under successive snowfalls, but when spring melts the snow they, too, will speak of her long sojourn here, as will the tufts of black-and-white fur snagged on the jagged entranceway to the den.

The giant panda and her cub are not the only creatures in this wild that must adjust their lives to survive the cruel winter season. The Tibetan snowcocks that live near the snowline and the ibis-bills seldom allow winter to drive them far from their summer haunts. The Thorald deer merely grow winter coats of hair twice the length of their summer ones. And the hardy muntjacs even choose this season to conduct their mating duels, like the musk deer, using sharp tusks instead of horns.

Pikas, snug in their burrows or in the crevices of rocks, thrive on the leafy harvests they have collected, coming out occasionally for a breath of fresh air. It is a leaner time for the moles and shrews, which do not hibernate but spend most of their time in their burrows where they live summer and winter, emerging only to hunt.

The wild boars also do not go any distance to escape the winter. When drifts pile up, making travel difficult, they wear narrow paths for themselves through the deep snow. They walk along these single file, moving either against or across the wind in their search for food. But most of the day they spend in the shallow beds they have dug for themselves and then lined with plant materials.

The blue sheep have only a short trek to make. When thick snows on the alpine meadows keep them from the grasses and lichen buried beneath, they descend to the edges of the brushlands. Here they can graze on the sere leaves and twigs of bushes and low trees.

But the white slopes are etched with the tracks of deer and

chamois and takin who travel greater distances. The graceful goral, which has shed its shaggy coat of hair for long fleece, has an especially hard time in winter. This little creature, so agile in the spring and summer, now moves with difficulty, foundering helplessly in new-fallen soft drifts. At such times it has to plod to some windswept rock to wait, marooned as though on an island, until wind and time have packed the snow and given it a hard crust that will bear its weight.

Only a few of the mountain's creatures can make an easy migration downward. The Lady Amherst pheasants and the Chinese hawfinches can take to their wings to reach the lower valleys where they stay during the bleakest months. Almost as free as the birds in their descent are the golden monkeys that swing through the tops of the trees.

The panda and her cub have to make the long trek on plodding feet over a treacherous landscape. The cub is now well-rounded and sleek, weighing more than fifteen pounds. His tail, which once seemed quite long, more and more resembles his mother's stubby one. Surer on his feet, he is even more active than before.

If there was any lesson to be learned from the tragic death of his sister he has not mastered it. More curious than ever about his surroundings, he frolics at the adult panda's side until some object attracts his attention. Then he's off at a tangent exploring it. The constant *hu hu hu* of his anxious mother rings out at intervals unheeded. Usually she has to go and bring him back bodily. Fortunately, the muscles in his legs are still weak, so he tires easily. He spends most of his time atop his mother's back.

The mother panda follows along the bank of the frozen stream, sensing from long experience that she will eventually come to the place where the water runs free again. The leafy green wilderness

Lady Amherst pheasant

through which she passed in the spring has been completely transformed. Snow and ice now seal over the trails through the bamboo thickets, turning them into long, luminous tunnels. One careless move or jostle and the roofs of those tunnels would come crashing down in a weight of ice and snow.

In other places the snow has bent the graceful bamboo fronds to the ground; ice has cemented them there, forming stiff icy hoops that bar her way. Sometimes she has to descend ice-sheathed slopes so steep that only her hairy soles keep her from falling. Sometimes her path leads across drifts so deep that she has to plow through them up to her belly. Where the snow is packed and firm she makes better time, striding along with a lopelike gait that, though swift, seems leisurely.

Blinding fogs and blizzards sweep down on her. Bitter winds howl from the high peaks that hover over the pandas with a rosy tinge in the afterlight of clear sunsets. Under the full moon the peaks gleam like burnished silver.

The mother stops often along the way to eat and rest and nurse the cub whose only food is still her milk. The little panda was more than three months old when he sprouted the first of his baby teeth—a molar. Now he has two other molars and a couple of front teeth. It will be another two to three months before he has all his teeth.

Though he hasn't enough teeth to chew with, the cub is beginning to show an interest in the bamboo fronds that his mother snaps off and discards. Practicing with his sixth claw, he is soon able to pick them up. While she eats he waves them about and occasionally sniffs at them. It is by its sense of smell that the panda distinguishes edible from inedible food, so the young cub in his play is learning an important skill too.

Along the way the sound of yelping comes once again to the

mother's ears, this time faintly from a distance. She seizes the cub and shimmies up the nearest tree, peering down in agitation, crying *hu hu hu.* The yapping is followed by several shots ringing out in the still air. Then silence returns again. The panda waits a little longer before she descends. She draws the cub to her breast and nurses it.

Unknown to her, some village hunters and their hounds have been tracking down the wild dog packs as they do every year in the winter, to keep their numbers under control. It is one of the few occasions on which men enter the preserve. Though they have come too late to save the little cub, other wilderness creatures will be safer now.

At last the giant panda reaches a place in the stream where the shell of ice is so thin that she can break through it and get to the water below. She bends her head to drink, and the little cub tries to mimic her. But he has no great love for water, and when his face gets drenched he almost loses his balance and tumbles in. He backs away from the bank, shaking his head in disgust.

A few days later the children of Kao Keng, snug in their fur-lined winter *shubas* and caps, spot the mother and cub at the near bend of the stream that flows through their village. The mother's gulping sounds of pleasure reach the children's ears as she drinks the cold water that rushes along free of ice here. The panda drinks and drinks until her belly swells like a balloon. Sated at last, she turns away, bloated with water. Slowly and awkardly, the cub at her heels, she moves into the bamboo thickets.

"The bear-cats are back. They're wintering with us again," the children cry.

53: The Downward Trek

7
Growing Up

THE VILLAGERS of Kao Keng see the two pandas occasionally during the rest of the winter. They wander through the tangle of bamboo thickets, sometimes in and sometimes out of the preserve. The climate is just right for them, though most human beings would find it too cold for comfort. There are frequent snowfalls, but they are not so deep as on the upper slopes. And though the wind has a biting chill and blizzards are common, they are not so fierce.

There are also days of sparkling sunlight when the little rodents of the wild venture from their burrows to get some fresh air, and the mother panda is able to augment her diet with a taste of jumping mouse or gray field rat. Her cub watches the tiny skittering creatures with interest. Sometimes he chases them across a clearing. But he's too awkward and they're too fast; he always ends up with empty paws.

Often during their treks mother and cub stop to rest. Noon usually finds them sprawled out in a cave or the hollow of a tree or atop a dead stump. But the little panda's siestas are never as long as his mother's. After a brisk game of roll and tumble about with him, she is ready for a good doze, but he doesn't seem at all sleepy.

For a while he sits motionless, contenting himself with shaking his head or his body back and forth in a kind of rhythm, to and fro, to and fro. But he soon tires of this exercise and wanders off to find a snow-covered incline, for he has discovered that it makes a much better toboggan slide than his mother's back. Bleating with satisfaction, he climbs to the top and rolls down sideways, climbs back, then rolls down again. Presently he discovers he can go much faster if he puts his paws over his eyes, curls up, and goes bouncing along like a ball. While only for fun now, this trick will be useful to him when, with his mother, he starts on the upward trek again.

Trees fascinate him. He mimics his mother when she scores the lower trunks with her claws. And he spends a lot of time lying on his back staring up at their leafy tops so high against the sky. One day, when he's five and a half months old, he spreads his arms and legs and digging his claws into the bark tries to shimmy up. His first try gets him only a couple of inches off the ground. But he keeps practicing over and over.

One day his mother wakes from a nap to find him nowhere in sight. *Hu hu hu,* she calls.

A small bleating, *eh eh eh,* answers from overhead. She looks up, and there is her cub perched in the fork of a branch six feet above her.

After that, it is impossible to keep him grounded. As he becomes more and more experienced, he mounts higher and higher, completely ignoring his mother's plaintive *hu hu*'s. Among the leafy branches he scampers up and down the limbs so far overhead that if he were to tumble, he would probably break his neck.

But he is not as independent as he seems. He is still easily

55: Growing Up

frightened. One day while he is in the trees a young eagle swoops down to see if he is the right size for eating. Though he is now much bigger than the eagle, it gives him such a scare that with a screech of terror he shimmies down the tree trunk, plops to the ground, and runs to his mother.

She clasps him in her arms, where he suckles for comfort. At more than six months of age he still depends on his mother's milk, though he now has all his baby teeth. But they're not strong enough or big enough to chew the tough bamboo. For that he will have to wait until his permanent teeth begin to arrive in another six months. Nevertheless, he begins to nibble at the leaves on the bamboo fronds with which he plays. And he practices licking himself clean afterward.

By the time spring comes to the valley in early April no one would recognize in the half-grown cub the tiny ratlike creature that was born seven months before. He is now three feet long and weighs about forty pounds. Despite his big-boned, chunky body, he is amazingly supple.

Spring brings a great delicacy for the pandas. Everywhere in the jungle new bamboo shoots are springing out of the wet earth from under the melting snow. They are tenderer than any other part of the bamboo, and even the panda cub can snack on them. Spring also brings green succulents along stream banks, which the cub can handle easily too. Spring makes possible another delicacy. As the sun grows warmer and the weather milder, the wild flowers begin bursting into bloom. Primrose and cowslips and fragrant lilies strew the meadows. Blue gentians cling to the banks of the stream, and purple violets glow in shady nooks. White butterflies are flitting everywhere. And the tribespeople's bees are humming loudly around their hives on the outskirts of the village.

Those hives, rich with stored honey, are a great temptation to the pandas. To them honey is one of the most wonderful delicacies on earth, and they will do almost anything to get at it.

The young panda's first introduction to honey is a mixed experience. One early morning he goes with his mother to the hives. Following her example, he pounces on a hive and scoops out the honeycomb, smearing the sweet, sticky mess over his paws and face as he smacks it down greedily. But he doesn't know enough to fling himself to the ground and roll about, batting off the bees. Several of them settle on his nose and sting him. With a shriek of pain he waves his paws wildly as his mother rushes to his aid.

Later, after the bees have calmed down and the honey is eaten, mother and cub go over their fur carefully, cleaning off every smear of the sweet, sticky stuff. The cub's painful experience with the bees doesn't dim the lure of honey for him; he comes back to the hives again and again. By now he has learned his lesson and is as quick as his mother to roll about and bat furiously at the angry insects, driving them off before they have a chance to sting.

One day, as mother and cub are loitering near the village, they pick up a tantalizing odor—the odor of roast lamb, more tempting even than the honey. It draws them out of the bamboo thickets and down to the village. They find it deserted, for the villagers have all gone off to gather the medicinal herbs that grow on the nearby cliffs.

The two pandas amble along the street toward the house from which the odor is coming. A push at the door, and it swings open for them. There on the kitchen table sits a leg of roast lamb, cooling while the owners are away.

57: Growing Up

The mother panda snatches it up in her jaws, and with the cub trailing her, leaves the kitchen and the village. The unfortunate householder returns just in time to see her disappear into the bamboo thickets, the roast clamped between her teeth. That leg of lamb, better than the taste of any vole, pika, or meadow mouse, disappears quickly.

But even honey and roast meat, delicious as they are, cannot hold the pandas in the valley when the season moves on and the days become uncomfortably warm for them. The time has come again to follow the tides of spring upward through the bamboo thickets.

8
The Separation

THE LAST TIME the panda cub journeyed through the bamboo wilderness all was deep in snow. Now a green jungle full of birds' songs and mating sounds surrounds him. New life is everywhere, the result of the previous fall's mating.

Golden monkey mothers clutch their tiny nursing babies to their breasts. Spotted fawns on wobbly legs suckle at their mother's teats. The musk deer fawns are especially frail creatures and cannot endure exposure to rain and wind. Every time bad weather threatens, their mothers must see that they are carefully sheltered.

The pale babies of the lesser pandas, born blind in their nests in hollow trees and rock crevices, will also be carefully watched over. In some three weeks' time their eyes will open. Presently they will be able to follow their parents around the wilderness in single file.

Female boars, too, each in her own secret birthing hollow padded with thick layers of herbiage, are giving birth. The tiny newborn pigs, five to six in a litter and covered only with scant white hairs, gather squealing at their mother's row of teats. Before

the year is over, all but two in every litter will have died from sudden freezes and drenching storms.

The young panda's curiosity is piqued by all these strange and interesting creatures. The appearance of some of them is frightening enough to make him keep his distance. When he and his mother meet the mighty takins on their trek upward he doesn't hesitate to roll downhill out of their way. He's curious about the furry little bear cubs that emerge from their caves with their parents at this time of year. But the adult black bears and especially the blue bears, gaunt and irritable from their long fasts, look too mean to approach.

It's different with a peculiar ball of tawny fur curled up and basking in the sun. The young panda can't resist going over and nuzzling it. The response is a snarl and a hiss. Out lashes a paw armed with sharp claws that rake across the cub's nose. He shrieks and swats back. But the tawny ball has unfolded itself into a lynx and streaks away unharmed. The young panda has learned one more painful lesson—curb curiosity, keep aloof from strangers.

He also learns to approach any suspicious object or animal from downwind, so that he can pick up the scent while not betraying his own presence. And he learns how to distinguish among the myriad sounds of the wilderness, for the hearing sense, which is acute in the panda, is as important to it as its sense of smell.

One day, for the first time after many tries, the panda cub manages to snare one of the small rodents that dart across his path. After that he is able to catch an occasional mouse or pheasant chick or pika. Gradually he overcomes his aversion to the rushing torrents he has to ford. And one day he lingers long enough in the shallows near the bank to scoop up a fish.

61: The Separation

Slowly he is beginning to wean himself. But until he can handle the tough bamboo stalks he will continue to nurse. And when he is hungry he always returns to his mother to be fed. Otherwise, he is more independent than ever.

Like any child, he invents all kinds of new games to play. He works small boulders out of cliff sides and rolls them over the ground. If they go down a slope, he chases after them faster and faster. When they come to a stop, he gives them another push.

In a similarly playful move he breaks off chunks of ice from shaded tree branches or rock shelves and swats them with his paw, sending them flying through the air. He chases the ice chunk, picks it up, and bats it again. With each bat it becomes smaller until finally it disappears in a puddle of water. Then he goes off to get himself another chunk.

Besides Roll the Boulder and Bat the Ice, the young panda does a lot of acrobatics. He practices standing on his big flattish head by leaning against a tree trunk and lifting his hind legs straight in the air. Soon he can do the trick without any support.

Standing on his head, he turns a somersault. At first his somersaults are awkward. But he becomes quite expert with practice and presently he can turn them one right after the other without stopping. Then he starts practicing cartwheels.

When summer is well launched on the lower slopes and the phalanxes of young bamboo sprouts have grown into tough bamboo culms, the pandas make their way to the high alpine meadows. This is a strange land to the cub. Here the newly arrived woolly lambs of the blue sheep, one to a ewe, are trailing their mothers. And the little fawns of the Thorald's deer are gamboling about on wobbly legs.

It is a peaceful scene, but the uneasiness that the adult panda feels troubles the young panda too. He becomes almost obedient as he follows his mother to the wet hollows and stream banks to browze on the young plants and tender roots that grow there.

Only once does he sight danger in the pale lithe form of the snow leopard stalking through the meadows. He catches a whiff of the killer scent and begins to shiver with fright, cringing against his mother for protection. He is as ready as she when the passing summer turns them back into the bamboo jungles.

Now the cub's independence is almost complete. Close to a year old, he weighs about eighty pounds, a fourth of the size he will eventually become. His permanent teeth are growing out. He is ready for his final lesson—learning how to eat the bamboo culms. Without this skill he can never survive in the wilderness.

At first he is very awkward at it. He rises on his hind legs and grabs at a stalk with his front paws. The resilient stalk sways out of his reach the first several times, and he topples over. But finally he manages to grasp the stem with both paws. He throws himself backward, keeping tight hold of the stem. Then he hooks one hind leg over it and twists around until he is on all fours astraddle it.

Slowly he works his way along it until he reaches the top. Then, holding the stem with one paw, he moves it to his mouth with the other and begins munching on the leaves. He contents himself with only the leaves at first. But before long he is learning to bite off and eat eighteen-inch sections of the culm just as his mother does.

This lesson learned, he is no longer dependent on her. He begins to stray farther and farther away. She lets him go without complaint, and though he may be absent for several days at a time, she no longer feels anxious about him. But she always welcomes him when he returns, clasping him to her and letting him nurse just as he did when he was very small. Actually it is only an affectionate gesture because now she has little nourishment to offer him. Her milk is drying up.

One day the young panda wanders off and does not return. He is on his own now and will spend the next five years of his life completing the education his mother began for him. His growing-up process will be a time of carefree wanderings. His playfulness will continue. Luminous moonlight will bring him out to feed and frolic in the bamboo glades, a black-and-white shadow flitting through an eerie world. Even during the dark nights he may rouse to eat and play for several hours before curling up for another nap.

But he will engage in some serious business, too. He will start staking out his own territory by scent marking. Rubbing his rump against tree trunks and boulders, he will leave behind his distinctive odor that will warn others to keep their distance. If, during the course of his scent marking, his presence is contested by other pandas or bears, he will fight to keep his place or move on. Finally he will have claimed his own particular section of mountain slope. In this section he will spend most of his adult life, overstepping its bounds only at the courting season when he is in search of a mate. Then he will add his fluting roar to the sounds of the wilderness every spring and fall, summoning a female to his side to create new life with her.

By this time he will have lost his playfulness and become a sedate adult, ambling and eating his way through the bamboo thickets. He will, one hopes, not fall prey to any of the predators that might possibly harm him. A greater threat to him would be some accidental fall from a cliff or a tree which, if serious enough, could cause brain damage resulting in convulsions and an early death. Severe infestations of pinworms could also weaken his

system, making him liable to pneumonia or inflammations of the stomach, ailments that also could shorten his life. But if he maintains his health, as pandas have a much better chance of doing in the wild away from civilization's germs, he could live for at least eighteen more years.

As for his mother, once her cub has gone for good, she no longer feels concern for it. In the forests she hears the fall courting roar of a male panda and lifts her head to listen. Once more her blood stirs. Once more she starts out on the old mating trek, leaving her scent as she goes.

The panda's year of mating, birth, growth, and separation has been but one in her species's infinite cycle of generations. Each year she will make her arduous journey up and down the mountains, face the harsh climate and the preying dangers that await her along the way, and if need be, fight to protect her own life and that of her cubs. It is a bitter and never-ending struggle, yet the mother panda will always be faithful to her summons. The survival of her ancient race depends on her.

66: The Separation

Epilogue

ACCORDING to Chinese zoologists, the panda's ancestor was a much smaller animal that prospered in the early Pleistocene era. The only fossils of this creature to be discovered to date were found in a cave in Liucheng in the far southern province of Kwangsi.

By the Middle Pleistocene, some 600,000 years ago, the small panda had developed into a much larger animal closely resembling today's giant panda. This panda was widely distributed throughout China; some of its bones have been discovered in the famous caves of Choukoutien outside Peking in northern China. Here they were mingled with those of Peking Man—one of China's Early Paleolithic peoples.

From the Yangtze River southward into Burma the giant panda was a common animal until the Late Pleistocene era. Then man began increasing in numbers, carving out more and more fields for himself from the wilderness. The climate also was changing. The bamboo forests on which the giant panda depended began to dwindle. The animal's range shrank until finally it was reduced to the cold rain forests of the far western mountains.

Europe first came to know about the giant panda in 1869 when a French missionary, Abbé Armand David, who was also a naturalist, went to the mountainous country of Szechuan Province to search for rare plant and animal life. A hunter brought him a dead panda, and he sent the skin and skeleton to a friend in France, naturalist Alphonse Milne-Edwards, for analysis.

Thus an argument started that has been going on for a century. To what family of animals does the giant panda belong?

Everyone agrees that it is a carnivore because, though its main diet is bamboo, it also eats some flesh. The ancestors of the modern carnivores are the miacids, small forest animals that lived some 60 million years ago. About 35 million years ago one branch of the miacids developed longer legs, larger brains, and sharp teeth with which they could tear flesh. This branch is called the canid branch and is the ancestor of the modern dog, fox, and wolf.

About 10 million years later, the canid carnivores began breaking up into branches. One branch developed handlike paws, supple limbs, and blunt teeth that they could chew vegetation as well as flesh. These were the procyonids. Animals such as the raccoon descended from them.

Several million years later, another branch split from the canids; this group was larger, developed heavier skeletons, and had big skulls. They also developed blunt teeth with which to chew vegetation. But their tails were much shorter and their legs heavier. These were the ursids, the bear family's ancestors.

In what family did the panda belong—the procyonids or the ursids? Today most zoologists have solved the question by giving the panda a special genus of its own because it has so many unique characteristics. This genus is called the *Ailuropoda*, which means "cat-footed." Some zoologists place the lesser panda in the giant panda genus. Others believe the lesser panda should remain in the raccoon family, and a very few want to give it a family of its own.

Therefore, the giant panda is scientifically classified as *Ailuropoda melanoleuca,* which means "the black-and-white cat-footed animal." The lesser panda is called *Ailurus fulgens,* or "fire-colored cat." But, of course, most people refer to them as the giant panda and the lesser panda.

The word *panda* comes from the little country of Nepal, which lies south of the Himalayan Mountains. *Panda* means "bamboo eater" and is the native name for the lesser panda, which frequents the forests of Nepal. When Westerners discovered the lesser panda, they adopted the Nepalese name for it. When they found the giant panda farther north, they simply called it the giant panda because it also was a bamboo eater. The Chinese themselves have several names for the panda: white bear, bear-cat, speckled bear, and monk bear. The last name was chosen because the animal likes to wander alone.

Despite all the names the panda has been given, it has never been well known in China. In the seventh century during the reign of the first T'ang Dynasty emperor, "white bear" skins are mentioned as having been among the gifts sent to the ruler of Japan along with two living white bears. But there is no proof that these white bears were pandas. They might have been polar bears obtained from the arctic regions far to the north. Or they might have been the Tibetan blue bear with its straw-colored pelt.

No further mention is made of the "white bear." But during the Ching Dynasty (1644–1911) panda skins were probably among the tributes sent to the emperors from the mountain tribespeople of Szechuan. If so, they were not highly prized by the royal court; the panda pelt was considered much too coarse for royal tastes. So the panda was relatively safe from predators until Western hunting expeditions began coming to the wilderness to bag this strange animal.

The first Western hunters to shoot a panda were the Roosevelt brothers, Theodore and Kermit, sons of American President Theodore Roosevelt. They brought the panda skin and bones back to America, and the animal was mounted and set up in the Field Museum in Chicago. This started the demand for mounted pandas in museums.

In 1936 Ruth Harkness, widow of the wild animal collector William Harvest Harkness, Jr., brought the first live panda to America. The live panda race was on. Soon the Chicago zoo had three live pandas; the Bronx zoo in New York City and the St. Louis zoo in Missouri obtained two each. Over in England the London zoo bought three pandas from a noted wild animal collector named Floyd Tangier Smith.

Since little was known about the care and transportation of captive pandas, many died after their capture, some even before they left Szechuan, others en route to their respective zoos. A large number of those that did survive the trip died prematurely in their new homes.

The two Bronx zoo pandas that had arrived in 1938 and 1939 were both dead by 1941. Zoo authorities immediately sent an order for two more to the West China Union University in Chengtu, capital of Szechuan Province. The university, which had begun to act as a panda clearinghouse, also received an order from Madame Chiang Kai-shek, wife of the Chinese ruler. She wanted to give a panda to the American people for their contributions to United China Relief. To obtain the three pandas the university gathered together seventy hunters who with forty dogs set out to search panda country. Despite their numbers and the large area they covered, they were able to capture only two pandas, which arrived at the Bronx zoo shortly after the bombing of Pearl Harbor.

At the end of World War II, with all three London zoo pandas dead, the British government appealed to the governor of Szechuan Province for two more pandas to take their places. Once again there was a massive search, this time with some two hundred peasants and professional hunters. They scoured panda country for two months before they succeeded in capturing one animal.

The Chinese began to realize that if they had to go to such extraordinary lengths, and take such a long time, to capture one panda, it could only mean that their prized animal, already rare, was dying out. On October 26, 1946, a Shanghai newspaper published this melancholy fact: "Szechuan's precious wildlife, the giant panda, has been hunted to the verge of extinction. This species that has been with us for so many thousands of years is bound to disappear and the world will never see it again."

In 1949, after the establishment of the People's Republic, the new government moved at once to save all its endangered species. The rarest of all, the giant panda, was first on the list. Several regions that the panda was known to frequent in numbers were set aside as preserves. Prohibitions were issued against hunting the panda, not only in these preserves but anywhere else it was to be found. Propaganda teams went to all the remote villages in panda country to explain the new regulations and to enlist the villagers' aid in protecting the panda.

A special bureau was established in Szechuan to advance on-the-spot investigations of the panda's habits in the wild. And though giant pandas can still be seen in zoos, collecting them is now the work of the government. Hunters can no longer go in at will and track them down for profit.

71: *Epilogue*

Those pandas that are captured are housed at an Animal Husbandry Station from which they are dispensed to zoos around the country. Peking Zoological Gardens got its first panda in 1956. Since then zoo pandas have steadily increased in China. Today there are some eighteen pandas in Chinese zoos. Zoologists at these zoos carry out continuous studies to determine the best methods of caring for the giant panda in captivity.

The panda has become more than a rare zoo animal. Today it is China's ambassador of goodwill, given to selected countries as a diplomatic gesture. No amount of money can buy a panda, but two have been presented to the Moscow zoo, three to zoos in North Korea and two to zoos in France. In 1972 two pandas arrived at Washington, D.C., following former President Nixon's visit to the People's Republic. And in 1975 two more pandas arrived at the zoo in Mexico City.

Meanwhile, in 1963 the first baby panda was born in a zoo—at the Peking Zoological Gardens. A year later a second arrived. Several others have been born since then.

In 1972 and 1973, survey teams of zoologists, making on-the-spot estimates of the numbers of pandas in Wanglang Preserve, determined that at least two hundred pandas are living in this area of 107 square miles. The villagers say this is a slight increase over the past.

But the giant panda's distribution far exceeds Wanglang Preserve. In 1940 a Chinese naturalist named Pen Hung-shou sighted it in Tsinghai Province in the Tibetan highlands. The alpine meadows where he saw it feeding and nursing its two cubs were 175 miles to the west of the nearest known panda country. Further investigation revealed that pandas were apparently not a rare occurrence there. Pen was told in the marketplace of Sining, capital of the province, that a panda skin was rarely seen for sale, not because it was scarce, but because it did not bring as high a price as the pelt of the blue bear.

The giant panda has also been sighted in the mountains of Shensi and Kansu provinces in the north and in those of Yunnan Province to the south. Altogether the area in which it has been seen covers thousands of square miles. No one knows for certain the exact number of pandas in this area, but now that hunting has been restricted, they should be increasing.

Whether or not the giant panda will continue to exist, however, depends on more than man. Several factors have to be taken into account. One is the very specialized diet on which the panda exists. In Wanglang Preserve, where for some twenty-five years no ax has been allowed, the trees have grown tall and luxuriant. If they are left uncut, will they choke out the bamboo thickets beneath them, thus starving out the pandas? On the other hand, will cutting them down to allow new forests to spring up aid or harm the panda? It is a problem that requires careful study, and Chinese zoologists are working on a solution.

Meanwhile, the pandas are safe—at least for the present. And there is good hope for the future now that man has taken an active interest in their preservation. This concern, added to the animal's own stubborn will to survive against incredible odds through the millennia, may preserve its beauty in the bamboo glades for years to come. And the black-and-white form that once awed simple tribespeople will continue to amble shadowlike through sunlit jungles, or frolic under the luminous moonlight—a living heritage from the world's ancient past.

73: Epilogue

Bibliography

BOOKS

ANDREWS, R. C. *Camps and Trails in China.* New York, 1918.

COLLINS, L. R., and PAGE, J. K., JR. *Ling-Ling and Hsing-Hsing.* New York, 1973.

CRESSEY, G. B. *Land of the 500 Million.* New York, 1955.

DAVIS, J. A. *Pandas.* New York, 1973.

FERGUSSON, W. N. *Adventure, Sport and Travel on the Tibetan Steppes.* New York, 1911.

FOX, H. M. *Abbé David's Diary.* Cambridge, Mass., 1949.

GRZIMEK, B. *Grzimek's Animal Life Encyclopaedia.* Vols. 7–13. Zurich, 1968; New York, 1972.

HARKNESS, R. *The Lady and the Panda.* London, 1938.

HEGNER, R. *Parade of the Animal Kingdom.* New York, 1935.

HOSIE, ALEXANDER. *Three Years in Western China.* London, 1890.

Larousse Encyclopedia of Animal Life. New York, 1967.

LITTLE, A. J. *Mount Omi and Beyond.* London, 1901.

LU, HSIANG-PIEN. *The Story of the Bear Cat.* Hongkong, 1974. Translated by M. Rau.

MORRIS, R., and MORRIS, D. *Men and Pandas.* London, 1966.

PERRY, RICHARD. *The World of the Giant Panda.* New York, 1969.

74: Bibliography

ROOSEVELT, T. and ROOSEVELT, K. *Trailing the Giant Panda.* New York, 1929.

SCHAEFER, E. *Ornithologische Ergebnisse Sweier Forschungsreisen nach Tibet.* Berlin, 1938. English excerpts.

SHABAD, T. *China's Changing Map.* New York, 1972.

WALKER, E. P. *Mammals of the World.* Vols. 1 and 2. Maryland, 1968.

WALLACE, H. F. *Big Game of Central and Western China.* London, 1913.

PERIODICALS

Acta Zoologica Sinica (Journal of the Peking Zoological Gardens). 1974. Includes the following articles about the panda, translated from the Chinese by M. Rau:

Anonymous. "Investigation into the Giant Panda's Propagation Methods and the Birth and Growth of Its Young."

———. "Rearing of the Giant Panda in the Zoo."

———. "Prevention and Cure of the Giant Panda's Diseases."

———. "Investigations into the Behavior of the Giant Panda in the Wanglang Preserve of Szechuan Province—Material Gathered by Expeditions to the Wanglang Natural Preserve of Szechuan."

———. "A Survey on the Giant Panda."

Chu Ching. "Concerning the Giant Panda's Classification—Peking Institute of Zoology Academia Sinica."

Pei Wen-chung. "Brief History of the Giant Panda."

Wang Tsiang-ke. "On the Taxonomic Status of Species, Geological Distribution and Evolutionary History of the Giant Panda."

Anonymous. "Baby Giant." *Time,* 1936.

———. "Mrs. Harkness and Her Panda." *Time,* 1937.

———. "In Pursuit of the Golden Monkey." *China Reconstructs* (Peking), 1960.

———. "In Search of the Panda." *Discovery,* 1933.

———. "Panda up a Tree." *Animal Kingdom,* 1942.

75: Bibliography

———. "Some Wild Animals in China." *China Reconstructs* (Peking), 1973.

National Zoological Park. "Information on Giant Pandas." Smithsonian Institute, Washington, D.C., 1975.

Roosevelt, K. "The Search for the Giant Panda." *Journal of the American Museum of Natural History*, 1937.

Sage, D. "In Quest of the Giant Panda." *Journal of the American Museum of Natural History*, 1935.

Sheldon, W. G. "Notes on the Giant Panda." *Journal of Mammalogy*, 1937.

Tangier-Smith, F. "Hunting the Panda." *Living Age*, 1937.

Wang Sung and Lu Chang-kun. "The Giant Panda." *China Reconstructs* (Peking), 1973.

Yao Chin-hua. "In the Homeland of the Giant Panda." *China Reconstructs* (Peking), 1974.

Index

Italicized numbers indicate illustrations in the text.

Acta Zoologica Sinica, vii
Ailuropoda, 68
  fulgens, 69
  melanoleuca, 69
Arrow bamboo, 4, 13
Altai Mountains, 22

Bear, 5, 17, 43, 61, 69
Beehives, 57
Bharal. *See* Blue sheep
Blue sheep, 5, 29, *31*, 35, 42, 49, 62
Boar, 35, 49
Bronx zoo, 70–71
Bubul, 17
Burma, 67

Canids, 68
Chamois, 42, 50
Chengtu, 70
Chiang Kai-shek, Madame, 70
Chicago zoo, 70
Chinacane, 4, 13
Chinese hawfinch, 50
Ching Dynasty, 69

Choukoutien caves, 67
Civet, 17
Cubs, giant panda
  appearance at birth, 33, *34*, 35, 36
  comparison of, 37–39
  death of, 44, *45*, 46
  eating habits, 36–37, 39, 52–53, 56–58, 62–64
  eyesight, 37
  hearing, 61
  playing, 38, 39, 50, 62
  predators on, 40, 41, 43–46, 63

David, Armand, 68
Deer, 29, 35, 42, 49, 62

Eagle, 21, 40, 56
Early Paleolithic era, 67
Early Pleistocene era, 67
Early Pliocene era, 29

Field Museum, 70
Field rat, 24
Flycatcher, 17
France, zoo in, 72

Giant panda
  birthing, 33, *34*, 35
  body postures, 6, 7, *11*, 15
  distribution, 3–5
  eating habits, 13–15, 38, *60*
  eyesight, 22
  genus and species, 17–18, 68–69
  mating, 7–12
  migration, 8, *9*, 20, 23–24, *27–31*, 48–52, 59
  pregnancy, 13, 31–32
  sleep habits, 15, 20, 36, 54
  see also Cubs, giant panda
Golden monkey, 25, 50, 59
Golden pheasant, 5
Goral, 5, 28, 34, 43, 50
Great tawny owl, 17

Harkness, Ruth, 70
Harkness, William Harvest, Jr., 70
Harvest mouse, 24
Himalayan black bear, 5, 17
Himalayan Mountains, 22, 69
Hunting, 42, 53, 70–71

Ibis-bill, 49

Japan, 69

Kansu Province, 73
Kao Keng, 4–5, 53–54
Kwangsi Province, 67

Lady Amherst pheasant, 5, 50, *51*
Leopard, 20
Lesser panda, *19*
  eating habits, 18
  genus and species, 68–69
  living habits, 5, 18, 36, 59
Liucheng, 67
Lynx, 5, 20, 40, 61

Meadow mouse, 21, 24
Mexico City zoo, 72

Middle Pleistocene era, 67
Milne-Edward, Alphonse, 68
Mole, 27, 42, 49
Monal pheasant, 20
Moscow zoo, 72
Muntjac, 20, 49
Musk deer, 20, 35, 49

Nepal, 69
Nixon, Richard M., 72
Nomads, 4
North Korea, zoo in, 72

Panda. *See* Giant panda, Lesser panda
Peking, 67
Peking Man, 67
Peking robin, *16*, 17
Peking Zoological Gardens, vii, 72
Pen hung-shou, 72
People's Republic of China, 4, 42, 71–72
Pheasant, 5, 20, 50, *51*
Pika, 21, 24, 42, 49
Procyonids, 68

Raccoon, 18, 68
Red deer, 35
Roosevelt, Kermit, 70
Roosevelt, Theodore (father), 70
Roosevelt, Theodore (son), 70

St. Louis zoo, 70
Sambar, 20
Schaefer, Ernest, viii
Serow, 5, 28
Shensi Province, 73
Shrew, 24, 42, 49
Smith, Floyd Tangier, 70
Snow leopard, 5, *21*, 22, 40, 63
Szechuan cuckoo, 17
Szechuan Province, vii-viii, 3–4, 42, 68, 70–71

Takin, 5, 25, 26, *27*, 43, 50
T'ang Dynasty, 69
Thorald's deer, 29, 49, 62
Tibetan blue bear, 5, 17, 69
Tibetan Mountains, 22
Tibetan snowcock, 5, 17, 49
Tibetans, 5, 42, 53–54

United China Relief, 70
Ursids, 68

Villagers, 42, 53–54
Vole, 21

Wanglang Preserve, viii, 4, 6, 72
Washington, D.C., zoo, 72
Water shrew mole, 27, 42
West China Union University, 70
Wild dog, 20, 22, 40, 42–46, 53
World War II, 71

Yangtze River, 67
Yunnan Province, 73

79: Index

MARGARET RAU was born and grew up in China, learning to speak Chinese before she spoke English. She later returned there for several years of extensive study of literature, history, culture, and language on the college level. On her most recent visit to the People's Republic of China in the fall of 1974, she gathered much of the research material for this book.

A photographer as well as author, Margaret Rau has written seven books for young people, including several geographical and historical studies of China and two full-length nature studies of penguins and musk oxen.

Ms. Rau is presently planning a trip to Australia and the South Pacific, where she will be doing research for a forthcoming book on kangaroos. She lives in Los Angeles, California.

EVA HÜLSMANN is a Swiss artist whose exquisite animal drawings have been admired in books and magazines both here and in Europe. She lives in Milan, Italy.